HOME MAINTENANCE

LOG BOOK

—THIS BOOK BELONGS TO—

Name : ....

Address : ....

....

Important *Contacts*

PROFESSIONAL NAME	PHONE	COMPANY NAME
Electrician		
Plumber		
HAVC		
Roofer		
Handyman		
Lawncare		
Sprinkler System		
Pool		
Hardscapes		
Windos/Siding		
Homewners Insurance		
Homewners System		
Police		
Fire		
Trash Removal		
Recycling		
Phone/Cable/Satellite		
Homewners Association		
Village/Township		
Voting Precinct		

Notes :

Important *Contacts*

PROFESSIONAL NAME	PHONE	COMPANY NAME
Electrician		
Plumber		
HAVC		
Roofer		
Handyman		
Lawncare		
Sprinkler System		
Pool		
Hardscapes		
Windos/Siding		
Homewners Insurance		
Homewners System		
Police		
Fire		
Trash Removal		
Recycling		
Phone/Cable/Satellite		
Homewners Association		
Village/Township		
Voting Precinct		

Notes :

Important *Contacts*

PROFESSIONAL NAME	PHONE	COMPANY NAME
Electrician		
Plumber		
HAVC		
Roofer		
Handyman		
Lawncare		
Sprinkler System		
Pool		
Hardscapes		
Windos/Siding		
Homewners Insurance		
Homewners System		
Police		
Fire		
Trash Removal		
Recycling		
Phone/Cable/Satellite		
Homewners Association		
Village/Township		
Voting Precinct		

Notes :

Important *Contacts*

PROFESSIONAL NAME	PHONE	COMPANY NAME
Electrician		
Plumber		
HAVC		
Roofer		
Handyman		
Lawncare		
Sprinkler System		
Pool		
Hardscapes		
Windos/Siding		
Homewners Insurance		
Homewners System		
Police		
Fire		
Trash Removal		
Recycling		
Phone/Cable/Satellite		
Homewners Association		
Village/Township		
Voting Precinct		

Notes :

Home Maintenance *Calender*

JANUARY

FEBRUARY

MARCH

APRIL

MAY

JUN

JULY

AUGUST

SEPTEMBER

OCTOBER

NOVEMBER

DECEMBER

Where *it is?*

Water Heater	Electrical Box

Hvac Units	Water Meter & Min Shut-off

Gas Meter & Maib Shut-Off	Sprinkler Controls

Smoke Detectors	Fire Extinguishers

Where *it is?*

Water Heater	Electrical Box

Hvac Units	Water Meter & Min Shut-off

Gas Meter & Maib Shut-Off	Sprinkler Controls

Smoke Detectors	Fire Extinguishers

Where *it is?*

Water Heater

Electrical Box

Hvac Units

Water Meter & Min Shut-off

Gas Meter & Maib Shut-Off

Sprinkler Controls

Smoke Detectors

Fire Extinguishers

Where *it is?*

Water Heater	Electrical Box

Hvac Units	Water Meter & Min Shut-off

Gas Meter & Maib Shut-Off	Sprinkler Controls

Smoke Detectors	Fire Extinguishers

Where *it is?*

Water Heater	Electrical Box

Hvac Units	Water Meter & Min Shut-off

Gas Meter & Maib Shut-Off	Sprinkler Controls

Smoke Detectors	Fire Extinguishers

Where *it is?*

Water Heater

Electrical Box

Hvac Units

Water Meter & Min Shut-off

Gas Meter & Maib Shut-Off

Sprinkler Controls

Smoke Detectors

Fire Extinguishers

Where *it is?*

Water Heater	Electrical Box

Hvac Units	Water Meter & Min Shut-off

Gas Meter & Maib Shut-Off	Sprinkler Controls

Smoke Detectors	Fire Extinguishers

Where *it is?*

Water Heater	Electrical Box

Hvac Units	Water Meter & Min Shut-off

Gas Meter & Maib Shut-Off	Sprinkler Controls

Smoke Detectors	Fire Extinguishers

Where *it is?*

Water Heater	Electrical Box

Hvac Units	Water Meter & Min Shut-off

Gas Meter & Maib Shut-Off	Sprinkler Controls

Smoke Detectors	Fire Extinguishers

Where *it is?*

Water Heater	Electrical Box

Hvac Units	Water Meter & Min Shut-off

Gas Meter & Maib Shut-Off	Sprinkler Controls

Smoke Detectors	Fire Extinguishers

Where *it is?*

Where *it is?*

Water Heater	Electrical Box

Hvac Units	Water Meter & Min Shut-off

Gas Meter & Maib Shut-Off	Sprinkler Controls

Smoke Detectors	Fire Extinguishers

Maintenance Service *Log*

Date	System / Appliance	Problem

Maintenance Service *Log*

Date	System / Appliance	Problem

Maintenance Service *Log*

Date	System / Appliance	Problem

Maintenance Service *Log*

Date	System / Appliance	Problem

Maintenance Service *Log*

Date	System / Appliance	Problem

Maintenance Service *Log*

Date	System / Appliance	Problem

Maintenance Service *Log*

Date	System / Appliance	Problem

Maintenance Service *Log*

Date	System / Appliance	Problem

Maintenance Service *Log*

Date	System / Appliance	Problem

Maintenance Service Log

Date	System / Appliance	Problem

Maintenance Service *Log*

Date	System / Appliance	Problem

Maintenance Service *Log*

Date	System / Appliance	Problem

Maintenance Service Log

Date	System / Appliance	Problem

Maintenance Service *Log*

Date	System / Appliance	Problem

Maintenance Service *Log*

Date	System / Appliance	Problem

Maintenance Service *Log*

Date	System / Appliance	Problem

Maintenance Service *Log*

Date	System / Appliance	Problem

Maintenance Service *Log*

Date	System / Appliance	Problem

Maintenance Service *Log*

Date	System / Appliance	Problem

Maintenance Service *Log*

Date	System / Appliance	Problem

Maintenance Service *Log*

Date	System / Appliance	Problem

Maintenance Service *Log*

Date	System / Appliance	Problem

Contrac Phone	How Was It Resolved	Satisfaction Rating

Contrac Phone	How Was It Resolved	Satisfaction Rating

Contrac Phone	How Was It Resolved	Satisfaction Rating
Contrac Phone	How Was It Resolved	Satisfaction Rating

Contrac Phone	How Was It Resolved	Satisfaction Rating

Contrac Phone	How Was It Resolved	Satisfaction Rating

Contrac Phone	How Was It Resolved	Satisfaction Rating

Contrac Phone	How Was It Resolved	Satisfaction Rating

Contrac Phone	How Was It Resolved	Satisfaction Rating

Contrac Phone	How Was It Resolved	Satisfaction Rating
Contrac Phone	How Was It Resolved	Satisfaction Rating

Contrac Phone	How Was It Resolved	Satisfaction Rating

Contrac Phone	How Was It Resolved	Satisfaction Rating

Contrac Phone	How Was It Resolved	Satisfaction Rating

Contrac Phone	How Was It Resolved	Satisfaction Rating

Contrac Phone	How Was It Resolved	Satisfaction Rating

Contrac Phone	How Was It Resolved	Satisfaction Rating

Contrac Phone	How Was It Resolved	Satisfaction Rating
Contrac Phone	How Was It Resolved	Satisfaction Rating

Contrac Phone	How Was It Resolved	Satisfaction Rating

Contrac Phone	How Was It Resolved	Satisfaction Rating

Contrac Phone	How Was It Resolved	Satisfaction Rating

Contrac Phone	How Was It Resolved	Satisfaction Rating

Contrac Phone	How Was It Resolved	Satisfaction Rating

Contrac Phone	How Was It Resolved	Satisfaction Rating

Contrac Phone	How Was It Resolved	Satisfaction Rating

Contrac Phone	How Was It Resolved	Satisfaction Rating
Contrac Phone	How Was It Resolved	Satisfaction Rating

Contrac Phone	How Was It Resolved	Satisfaction Rating
Contrac Phone	How Was It Resolved	Satisfaction Rating

Contrac Phone	How Was It Resolved	Satisfaction Rating

Contrac Phone	How Was It Resolved	Satisfaction Rating

Contrac Phone	How Was It Resolved	Satisfaction Rating

Contrac Phone	How Was It Resolved	Satisfaction Rating

Contrac Phone	How Was It Resolved	Satisfaction Rating

Contrac Phone	How Was It Resolved	Satisfaction Rating
Contrac Phone	How Was It Resolved	Satisfaction Rating

Contrac Phone	How Was It Resolved	Satisfaction Rating

Contrac Phone	How Was It Resolved	Satisfaction Rating

Contrac Phone	How Was It Resolved	Satisfaction Rating

Contrac Phone	How Was It Resolved	Satisfaction Rating

Contrac Phone	How Was It Resolved	Satisfaction Rating

Contrac Phone	How Was It Resolved	Satisfaction Rating

Contrac Phone	How Was It Resolved	Satisfaction Rating

Contrac Phone	How Was It Resolved	Satisfaction Rating

Project *Planner*

Name Of Project

Project Description :

Completion Date **Total Budget**

Materials List	Expented Cost	Actual Cost
Total Cost		

Services	Expented Cost	Actual Cost
Total Cost		

Project Notes :

Project *Planner*

Name Of Project

Project Description :

Completion Date

Total Budget

Materials List	Expented Cost	Actual Cost
Total Cost		

Services	Expented Cost	Actual Cost
Total Cost		

Project Notes :

Project *Planner*

Name Of Project

Project Description :

Completion Date   **Total Budget**

Materials List	Expented Cost	Actual Cost
Total Cost		

Services	Expented Cost	Actual Cost
Total Cost		

Project Notes :

Project *Planner*

Name Of Project

Project Description :

Completion Date		Total Budget	

Materials List	Expented Cost	Actual Cost
Total Cost		

Services	Expented Cost	Actual Cost
Total Cost		

Project Notes :

Project *Planner*

Name Of Project

Project Description :

Completion Date **Total Budget**

Materials List	Expented Cost	Actual Cost
Total Cost		

Services	Expented Cost	Actual Cost
Total Cost		

Project Notes :

Project *Planner*

Name Of Project

Project Description :

Completion Date

Total Budget

Materials List	Expented Cost	Actual Cost
Total Cost		

Services	Expented Cost	Actual Cost
Total Cost		

Project Notes :

Project *Planner*

Name Of Project

Project Description :

Completion Date   **Total Budget**

Materials List	Expented Cost	Actual Cost
Total Cost		

Services	Expented Cost	Actual Cost
Total Cost		

Project Notes :

Project *Planner*

Name Of Project

Project Description :

Completion Date | **Total Budget**

Materials List	Expented Cost	Actual Cost
Total Cost		

Services	Expented Cost	Actual Cost
Total Cost		

Project Notes :

Project *Planner*

Name Of Project

Project Description :

| **Completion Date** | | **Total Budget** | |

Materials List	Expented Cost	Actual Cost	Services	Expented Cost	Actual Cost
Total Cost			**Total Cost**		

Project Notes :

Project *Planner*

Name Of Project

Project Description :

Completion Date   **Total Budget**

Materials List	Expented Cost	Actual Cost
Total Cost		

Services	Expented Cost	Actual Cost
Total Cost		

Project Notes :

Project *Planner*

Name Of Project

Project Description :

Completion Date   **Total Budget**

Materials List	Expented Cost	Actual Cost
Total Cost		

Services	Expented Cost	Actual Cost
Total Cost		

Project Notes :

Project *Planner*

Name Of Project

Project Description :

Completion Date

Total Budget

Materials List	Expented Cost	Actual Cost
Total Cost		

Services	Expented Cost	Actual Cost
Total Cost		

Project Notes :

Project *Planner*

Name Of Project

Project Description :

Completion Date **Total Budget**

Materials List	Expented Cost	Actual Cost
Total Cost		

Services	Expented Cost	Actual Cost
Total Cost		

Project Notes :

Project *Planner*

Name Of Project

Project Description :

Completion Date

Total Budget

Materials List	Expented Cost	Actual Cost
Total Cost		

Services	Expented Cost	Actual Cost
Total Cost		

Project Notes :

Project *Planner*

Name Of Project

Project Description :

Completion Date   **Total Budget**

Materials List	Expented Cost	Actual Cost
Total Cost		

Services	Expented Cost	Actual Cost
Total Cost		

Project Notes :

Project *Planner*

Name Of Project

Project Description :

Completion Date   **Total Budget**

Materials List	Expented Cost	Actual Cost
Total Cost		

Services	Expented Cost	Actual Cost
Total Cost		

Project Notes :

Project *Planner*

Name Of Project

Project Description :

Completion Date   **Total Budget**

Materials List	Expented Cost	Actual Cost
Total Cost		

Services	Expented Cost	Actual Cost
Total Cost		

Project Notes :

Project *Planner*

Name Of Project

Project Description :

| **Completion Date** | | **Total Budget** | |

Materials List	Expented Cost	Actual Cost
Total Cost		

Services	Expented Cost	Actual Cost
Total Cost		

Project Notes :

Project *Planner*

Name Of Project

Project Description :

Completion Date | **Total Budget**

Materials List	Expented Cost	Actual Cost
Total Cost		

Services	Expented Cost	Actual Cost
Total Cost		

Project Notes :

Project *Planner*

Name Of Project

Project Description :

Completion Date	**Total Budget**

Materials List	Expented Cost	Actual Cost
Total Cost		

Services	Expented Cost	Actual Cost
Total Cost		

Project Notes :

Project *Planner*

Name Of Project

Project Description :

Completion Date **Total Budget**

Materials List	Expented Cost	Actual Cost
Total Cost		

Services	Expented Cost	Actual Cost
Total Cost		

Project Notes :

Project *Planner*

Name Of Project

Project Description :

Completion Date

Total Budget

Materials List	Expented Cost	Actual Cost
Total Cost		

Services	Expented Cost	Actual Cost
Total Cost		

Project Notes :

Project *Planner*

Name Of Project

Project Description :

Completion Date   **Total Budget**

Materials List	Expented Cost	Actual Cost
Total Cost		

Services	Expented Cost	Actual Cost
Total Cost		

Project Notes :

Project *Planner*

Name Of Project

Project Description :

Completion Date   **Total Budget**

Materials List	Expented Cost	Actual Cost
Total Cost		

Services	Expented Cost	Actual Cost
Total Cost		

Project Notes :

Project *Planner*

Name Of Project

Project Description :

Completion Date

Total Budget

Materials List	Expented Cost	Actual Cost
Total Cost		

Services	Expented Cost	Actual Cost
Total Cost		

Project Notes :

Project *Planner*

Name Of Project

Project Description :

Completion Date   **Total Budget**

Materials List	Expented Cost	Actual Cost
Total Cost		

Services	Expented Cost	Actual Cost
Total Cost		

Project Notes :

Project *Planner*

Name Of Project

Project Description :

Completion Date **Total Budget**

Materials List	Expented Cost	Actual Cost
Total Cost		

Services	Expented Cost	Actual Cost
Total Cost		

Project Notes :

Project *Planner*

Name Of Project

Project Description :

Completion Date | | **Total Budget** |

Materials List	Expented Cost	Actual Cost	Services	Expented Cost	Actual Cost
Total Cost			**Total Cost**		

Project Notes :

Project *Planner*

Name Of Project

Project Description :

Completion Date | **Total Budget**

Materials List	Expented Cost	Actual Cost
Total Cost		

Services	Expented Cost	Actual Cost
Total Cost		

Project Notes :

Project *Planner*

Name Of Project

Project Description :

Completion Date

Total Budget

Materials List	Expented Cost	Actual Cost
Total Cost		

Services	Expented Cost	Actual Cost
Total Cost		

Project Notes :

Project *Planner*

Name Of Project

Project Description :

Completion Date | **Total Budget**

Materials List	Expented Cost	Actual Cost		Services	Expented Cost	Actual Cost
Total Cost				**Total Cost**		

Project Notes :

Project *Planner*

Name Of Project

Project Description :

Completion Date

Total Budget

Materials List	Expented Cost	Actual Cost
Total Cost		

Services	Expented Cost	Actual Cost
Total Cost		

Project Notes :

Project *Planner*

Name Of Project

Project Description :

Completion Date   **Total Budget**

Materials List	Expented Cost	Actual Cost
Total Cost		

Services	Expented Cost	Actual Cost
Total Cost		

Project Notes :

Project *Planner*

Name Of Project

Project Description :

Completion Date | **Total Budget**

Materials List	Expented Cost	Actual Cost
Total Cost		

Services	Expented Cost	Actual Cost
Total Cost		

Project Notes :

Project *Planner*

Name Of Project

Project Description :

Completion Date   **Total Budget**

Materials List	Expented Cost	Actual Cost		Services	Expented Cost	Actual Cost
Total Cost				**Total Cost**		

Project Notes :

Project *Planner*

Name Of Project

Project Description :

Completion Date   **Total Budget**

Materials List	Expented Cost	Actual Cost
Total Cost		

Services	Expented Cost	Actual Cost
Total Cost		

Project Notes :

Project *Planner*

Name Of Project

Project Description :

Completion Date		**Total Budget**	

Materials List	Expented Cost	Actual Cost		Services	Expented Cost	Actual Cost
Total Cost				**Total Cost**		

Project Notes :

Project *Planner*

Name Of Project

Project Description :

Completion Date　　　　　　**Total Budget**

Materials List	Expented Cost	Actual Cost
Total Cost		

Services	Expented Cost	Actual Cost
Total Cost		

Project Notes :

Project *Planner*

Name Of Project

Project Description :

Completion Date   **Total Budget**

Materials List	Expented Cost	Actual Cost
Total Cost		

Services	Expented Cost	Actual Cost
Total Cost		

Project Notes :

Project *Planner*

Name Of Project

Project Description :

Completion Date   **Total Budget**

Materials List	Expented Cost	Actual Cost
Total Cost		

Services	Expented Cost	Actual Cost
Total Cost		

Project Notes :

Project *Planner*

Name Of Project

Project Description :

Completion Date **Total Budget**

Materials List	Expented Cost	Actual Cost
Total Cost		

Services	Expented Cost	Actual Cost
Total Cost		

Project Notes :

Project *Planner*

<table>
<tr><td>Name Of Project</td><td></td></tr>
</table>

Project Description :

<table>
<tr><td>Completion Date</td><td></td><td>Total Budget</td><td></td></tr>
</table>

Materials List	Expented Cost	Actual Cost
Total Cost		

Services	Expented Cost	Actual Cost
Total Cost		

Project Notes :